Anton G. Leitner

SELECTED POEMS
1981–2015

Translated from the German
by Richard Dove, Paul-Henri Campbell,
Anatoly Kudryavitsky and Yulia Kudryavitskaya

ſV

SurVision Books

First published in 2018 by
SurVision Books
Dublin, Ireland
www.survisionmagazine.com

Copyright © Anton G. Leitner, 2018
Translations © Richard Dove, 2018
Translations © Paul-Henri Campbell, 2018
Translations © Anatoly Kudryavitsky
and Yulia Kudryavitskaya, 2015, 2018

The poet's photograph by Volker Derlath, Munich
Design © SurVision Books, 2018

ISBN: 978-1-9995903-8-3

Acknowledgements

Grateful acknowledgement is made to the editors of the
following, in which a number of these poems originally
appeared: "Buoys Whisper", "A Short Round-the-World Trip
with F.", "First Aid", "Mr. Finally": *Coloured Handprints: 20
German-Language Poets,* Dedalus Press, Dublin, Ireland, 2015.

CONTENTS

I. 1981–1990

II. 1991–2000

III. 2001–2015

* Translated by Paul-Henri Campbell
** Translated by Anatoly Kudryavitsky and Yulia Kudryavitskaya
The rest of the poems translated by Richard Dove

1981–1990

Time, Sick

The clock
was drunk
and swung her
pendulum
striking three
frontally
into my face.

The clock-hand
threw up,
time
threw up its hands,
surrendered to lying vertigo,
and on
I ticked.

Re Unification

Some smoke re
turns to its
fire.

Playing the Man Not the Ball

War, our
Best

Heads
Once again

Don't
Roll

Out of
Play

Offside-
Trap

Dark Andechs Feeling

Beer and
Believe me

Intoxicated
I see

Angels
Puke.

Thoughts, Feverish

It can't be
What you —

But it is
What we —

And yet
It was —

But it is
No longer.

Popular Festival

When into the tankards
The noses
Grow.

At Night

The lights are going on
in the houses.

Beyond the windows
who would divine
the hammer-blows
on the heads
of happily married folk.
But spurious romantic gestures
aren't genuine either:
married life is not
a crime movie.
Though the murderer
does still at times
emerge from the wings
dressed in a white shirt,
a stain on his waistcoat
(clamping a knife
in between
his teeth).

Surprises
are lurking all around you.

Picked Up in the Boughs

We couple more often
Than full moon and twigs.

Watch carefully through this wooden eye!
Call out those copulating

In mink, and laugh
Till their backs are rounded like branches.

Summer by the River Isar

Drowsiness
between the
legs is a
raspberry ice-cream
from the Italian
round the corner.

"Cool, baby, cool"
the newspaper
says, but
who the hell knows
of sandals
to which the
sweat sticks
from however perfect
a foot.

The sun
is tanning the
spat-out
chewing gum
after a luxury
wallow in oil.

Who thinks of
sleep at this
time when what counts
is sacrificing one's body
on the grill
for these looks.

Ancien Régime

Madam,
your poise
is so aristocratic.

Even at table
you don't mince
matters, eat
no mince at all,

keeping
religiously
to your diet.

On your face
between two lines
of wrinkles
is written
the word
"autumnal";
it sports
a pointed plume
on its hat.

Now and again
you shed
years.

Buoys Whisper

The moon still looks
black.

The salt tosses around
restlessly.

Somebody starts a fire
on top of a hill.

The scenery
burns out.

The waves of the morning
crash
upon the day.

Step Forward, Step

My great-grandfather Josef
(one thing he did
was bronze-plate
the harnesses
of the brewery nags
at the *Oktoberfest*)
still kept
a sow
in the bustle of Munich's district called Au,
Mary-Help-Street Number 4.

Through a hole
in the wall
the sow crept
to Alois Birk
on the corner of Spring Street /
Mary-Help-Street
(on the side,
this chap traded cloth at the fair
and otherwise collected
old paper
during the year).

They divided up
the sow fifty-fifty
on that occasion.

A couple of houses further down
is where I, the great-grandson,

am now living
along with my rat
(my freelance glances
sometimes still brush
the harnesses of the
brewery nags
from the Oktoberfest.)

My Ratman
has no hole in the wall
to get through to my neighbours
(his hearing is poor,
she can't see any
longer.
They live a thoroughly modern life:
two pensioners cohabitating.
Now and then
they both still emerge
from their home.)

My sow
who's a rat
resides in the toilet.
By now my fine beast
has already got used
to the sound
of flushing.

Ricky

Ricky
was a classmate of mine.

While a student he walked
towards the subway
because he was stoned
and searching
for Jesus
in the ash container.

He got torn to pieces.

I came across him
recently
(after he'd been buried
in Munich's
old northern cemetery)
at the uni
in the *Ludwigstrasse*.

I recognised his cha-cha-cha gait
and he saw it was

me. *Life's not*
that bad
in hell, mate
he remarked,
and his teeth were yellow,
and he grinned

as he used to do
before Latin classes.

And once again
he was smoking a joint
as he used to do
after Ancient Greek.

Christmastide

I.

History,
In the night
Of his birth,

Does not take another
Retrograde step. Some
Found their

Dream illumined
By electric
Light.

Then the candles
Burned
To the rhythm of the

Programmed
Timer
And no honey

Dripped
From Jesse's
Tree.

II.

Once a year
The moon turns two
Benevolent blind

Eyes, bestowing
Its light upon
A star.

Three men
Find the road
To the end

Of the night. No
Smoke can
Deceive them.

Their gift
Is a cross
Which grows

With the child.
One for all
And all

Against him.
How it ends,
We all know.

Lover Boy 86

Those were the
days when the
nuclear sirens whined
themselves hot just practising
and I got through
two campaigns
in Russia
on my school-bench
before becoming enamoured
of John F.
who kindly dropped raisins
after the bombs
and gave me marshmallows
and gum-gum
bullets
to feed my army
of plastic
MGs,
and counted on
Baader and Ulrike,
and went a
little crazy
and fiddled my Castro
a little,
before meeting Grace,
my loyal spouse,
who had kids with me,
a model
homemaker,

who only demonstrated
her sparkling cooking range
before kindred spirits
and who was a fellow traveller
of doves of peace
which I was compelled to grind
into grit
rub dry
in jute sacks
until our daily
roast got finally spirited up
and the sack
was left
as my suit.

Early Morning Pint

In the dovecote
The beaks
Are foaming

Angels

Come down from on high
Are we,
Skyscrapers,
The gondola's
Dangling there
In limbo
Behind the glass,
Hello, is someone
There
Below us and in our midst is no
Humane human
Let us, hosanna,
Remain in excelsis.

First-Term Students

How we quaked
When your period was late,
Even later, and still refused to come –
Every day from the frying-pan into the fire
With thoughts of
Abortion in Bavaria
All's well with the world
Proclaims the father of our nation
IN PEACE AND FREEDOM
LIFE IS AN INDISPENSABLE
COMPONENT PART OF THE COMMUNITY
IN THE SERVICE OF HUMANITY
We had these words in our noddles
And thought "sounds good"
That man needs men
Who'll stand up for his values
If push comes to shove, he'll help us
He's got a big heart which beats
For the kids in the overcrowded
Lecture-hall you said
I'M TOO YOUNG and
MY BELLY BELONGS TO
God, what could I do
Except wait and lift
The phone your voice
THE DIE IS

Yours Truly

Between us everything's over
Ly normal, that ends well
All
As well the exchange of long-proffered
Endearments will be refunded
In return for costs totalling

Further by return of post, you'll restitute:
1 set of cross-country skis
1 set of cross-country skiing boots
1 set of ice-skates
1 set of white sandals (in the basement)
1 set of pyjamas
1 belt (ocre-coloured) (in the green cupboard)
1 book (Hite Report)
1/2 of a legal commentary (Constitution) 99 pounds, 99.

1991–2000

The Heads Are the Tails and the Tails Are the Heads

Vote for the lesser evil, you lot,
The unity of the sausage
In the maw of the sow
Heads wins
The black conservative tails
In blazing socialist
Red

A Short Round-the-World Trip with F.

Everything I need
Around me: you, I mean,
My foothold. But join me
In the revolving loop.
It is in rotation that we
Describe ourselves correctly:
A man and a woman.
Until the carousel comes to a halt
We will stand firm.

Dirge

for Käte Wölpl, called Mädi
(1904–1993)

Nothing's missing. You
Are. You're missing.

Your laughter's missing.
In my ear the two words:

"Heeey?" "Crazy!"
Long-drawn-out, amazed –

And always there in the thick,
in the quick, of your grandchildren's

Lives. No cross
Stands for that: the last

Place is home to nobody.
Eighty-four-one-two-

Nine-two-six
For the moment the person

You're calling can't
Be reached can't be reached.

Any
Longer.

35

East-West Divide

Border-guard-SS tommyrot rotting card-
Board target camera on, life
Is a film, the sequence
Of images a question
Of camera-angle: infrared transforms
Night into day, pan, e.g. the woman
Over there left in the sights
German or Polish cit-
Ting duck with her baggage or rather plastic-
Bags on a bike is skillfully
Hiding her wealth, Capital
Is fleeing by road and the State
Here too is missing
Out. "Get these refugees home
Or, if not, get them to pay!" Tax-free bare
Minimum as social means
Of proof discarded I-
Cons, quasi-official news
Situation: "so-called local border
Traffic – legal / illegal trans-
Gressions ad-
Missible catalogue of
Measures ... envisaged
Opening op-
Timised ... Goodnight good neigh
Bourly austerity

Package ... all else in-
Applicable in-
Vented, in-
Decent lying stink" un-
Quote

Holy Year

That smells of
Mint. There's no cement

Left, hole
Gaping in tooth. Anti-

Biotic thanks:
Chastity

Belt. Shingly rose, Mary
Please an urge-

Nt prayer for us
Poor sinners now

And without
A rubber. The immaculate

Sheath
Bursts. Bang.

Don't Shout

Like that! Tune into
The quiet of
Things.

Blackbird Killing Fields: Battle for Bare

Vival. Sir
Vival. We. The

Majority. Silence.
Wage war

In our suits. Our
Ties drag

Bombs. Our
Cuff-links

Skew-whiff. Heads
Limp on plunging para-

Chutes. Bread for
Cash. Vision

Of deficiency as
St. Francis of

Havenot-
Anything-to-give-away.

Where are the
Ruskies, coming

Later. Maybe on the
Never-never. Count to ten

Million dollars. Immediate
Aid. What that

Means: cost
Containment. Watch

Out you lot!
It's

Starting.

Snow, Man

What you live today
You remember

Tomorrow. Tomorrow,
Snow will fall. The day

After, melt.
In her

Arms.

Simple Arithmetic

Is one coming round
The bend, or

None? If
Two add up

In the bend,
That's one divided

By two equals
Half a

Life.

Dual Citizen

Prison. Green card. *Don't say*
Anything, each

Expression is a
Copy is an

Original. And can be used
Against. Three

Persons, two
Passports. Globali-

Syrup, great big welcoming
De. Port. A-

Tion station. Marching, marching
Music, played

Backwards: Home into Hitler's
Reich! "She tends

Home and hearth and he
Tends her." Wrong.

"We, the cloned
Sheep let the

Shepherds move on." Correct.
To say Good

Bye makes you new
Friends. Two stars

World Famine
Aid. "Did the last

Fag taste tangy, Mr.
Bits and Ms.

Bytes, let the best
Brains carry on

Storming in the
Name of

Germany, I implore you
Stay

Online."

Pars pro toto

Shiny eye
of the parrot

of the fish: his
mortality outlasts

life a few
hours.

(Effigy of the last
surprise.) Maybe

the favorite dish
of a highly

born man
whose stomach

growled in expectation.
A quick prayer

(formulaic), one or two
bites from the Atlantic

taken. Forever
the gaping open

mouth as expression
for eternal

youth. Reoccurring
memory: "Thanks, the

head returns
back into the salt."

Can I Boil (You Too?)

Grills himself.
The flesh wafts

Into a nose.
But a belly

Button pierced
At fifteen

Pregnant. Holy
Virgin, pray

For us medium
Or with the fat

Running through. What
Makes the table groan

Makes weary men
Sprightly. Not so

Splayed, stiltedly displayed.
Everyone gets his

Best part bitten o-
Ff.

CV, Mine

Is there any truth
in the matter. Water

carrying thin
paper, a

rumor: air
dried out

throat. Song-
bird! Crazy

Beppi
fizzy

tablet. Dis-
solving, there

the rising
base

re-
venue.

Marital Hygiene

One brain
Half burnt up.

The better
Half embarks alone

On its whore-
lday.

The Ocean Sees

The land with other
Eyes. (Its gaze wanders

From blue to yellow to
Green.) A shifting

Pillow for a quiet
Night in a lap.

Pizzeria Mamma Mia

Petite
Patroness from
Cuba: puff

Pastry with swiv-
Elling hips, open
Fire. Sweet

Meats, menu
Turned on its
Head. Southern

Fruit first
Then pizza
House-

Style. "I
Don't really know
Señor

Where the in-
Gredients come from but
They taste

Good, my husband
Is from Mi-
Lan, has Palermo

In his blood, when we quarrel
They all hear everything."
First Fuerte

Ventura. One
Year without
Rain, second

Choice: Saint
Andrew on the
Indolent isle La

Palma. Bananas
Or the crooked
Church San Andrés

Apóstol. Thick
Walls as protection
Against the pirates. The

Flight of the
Fatties from
Fat

Cigars. Week-long
Beard, dirty
Shirt peeping from

Open pants
God's
Garden with turn

Stile, run to ruin
Seesaw and
Swing. Naked

Thighs, the
First day without
A guest on the floor

The blood-drenched-red trousers:
Go to hell
Where mafiosi are munching peperoncini!

Prayers help
Little, Tourists
Just eat fish

And no fish is leaping
From the pan
As a fillet. "Mamma

Mia, once *Four*
Seasons for five
Island-dwellers! And

One free
Drink. They work up
An appetite

Here and
Sate their hunger
At home."

Life

Drawn from life:
The voice of the

Dead on
Answer

Phone. A
Slice of one's own

Childhood un-
Wound. Over-

Written.

2001–2015

Hello Again, the Baby Is Hollering

Hello again, / the baby is hollering
To the mother, / and mother to father /
The baby is hollering, / and father to baby, /
But the baby keeps right on hollering Hallo
Dad Hallo mum Hallo, / Hallo
dad hollers back, / mum
Hollers back Hallo, / hell yeah! hollers the
Baby, Hallo, / Hallo's just an echo / thinks
Dad: am I the baby, / thinks the
Baby: I am mum, / the baby
Is dad, / is mum eating the baby
Skin halo and all / the belly rumbles /
Again in the belly the baby hollers
Hallo Hallo / but hell, oh! I
Need to / says mum, / give birth / says
The baby, / and dad just watches and
Once again abseils down the umbilicus, / cord
Tears, / the baby can already
Holler, / my God it's really
Hollering / Hallo, / Hallo the midwife hollers
Back again, / the baby is
Hollering.

Toilet, Lady

Dirty
Not make
Thankya
Dirty
Not you
Thankya
Dirty
Make
Thankya
I go clean
Thankya
Make
Must go clean
Thankya

O Leap

In the o
rig in
an o
vum leapt out.

For Sale

One decides upon departure
into a different zone
—Karl Krolow

Even the closed
Window does not keep

Shut, the coast
Is swept by voluble

Wind. We exchange
Words, e.g. about

The salinity
Of the air or

Duck liver pâté.
Whoever caresses

Our daily
Bread so gently

The radio chants
Love in every

Position. Please pull
The plug and

Hang the sign
Out.

First Aid

Is the patch stuck
To the brain or

The brain to
The patch?

Ask away
So you can

Learn
Something

And keep the
Brain

Separate from
The patch.

Big Break in Winter

Out of the gaps
In the manhole covers
White fumes are

Straining. Paper
Is writhing on the ground,
Wishing it were

Back round a
Sweet which was
Melting away on someone's

Tongue. I take
A deep draw and let
Rings a-

Scend. Ma's
Bread goes on freezing
In its rucksack.

A Bothering Thing

Two people
On the bench; she's
On the phone – with whom?

It's clear now that my child
Will be a girl,
I'm positive.

Not the father, he thinks,
And goes: *Your shoe lace*
Is undone.

Mr. Finally

Rushes home
After office hours.

I won't take
Advantage

Of you losing ground
To me,

He says
Just this

And nothing
Else

A skeleton
In a suit

Carrying
Between the files

Two layers
Of sausages and cheese

Wholemeal
Freak-out.

Jobs for the Boys

On the super
Visory

Board
Bored

Vice
Nods all items

Through.
Super, warm thanks. No

Need for change.

Burial_costs.xls

On balance,
A good

Deal:
Even the postage

Paid by the
Twice-removed

Relatives,
He tumbled away from his loved-ones

Out of bed to the dead
With coffee and

Curses cost-effective fun-
Ereal

Feast, a
Pint per

Thank God
Preserve

Hops and
Salt in the

Tear-
Ink-jet

Glands clogged up
The card with the

Dead-man's face smudged
Already at

First glance
A warmhearted

Fellow with a good
Disposition and firm

Fixed-interest
Securities when

Called, at once,
Two thousand and

Six euros
For the child

Of each and every
Child: *It's more*

Blessed to give
Than

Bio, Rhythm

The little gust
Hugs beech-

Leaves
Which curl and

Whirl in
Free

Fall.

Churchwood, Untended

Little
Light

In the shadow
The Lord casts

Adders
Are thriving

Adders' tongue
Ferns.

Hot Flushes

All over, the city's
Tearing deep trenches. New long-distance
Heating network at sweltering

Temperatures. How the
Times change: Cap-
Ital of the Nazi Movement 1935

Cool Centre for Bike-Peddlers 2010. Look
Ole Sturdycalves is lugging
His entire brood in the trail-

Er and meanwhile
The small fry are sweating
Themselves silly. Even the pensioner

Chieftain in his blue mocassins
Is waving a dinky handbag
In front of the lady's loo in the park-

Ing lot, the grey mouse with the red
Frame glasses, original Sioux
Branding power, seems relieved when she

Is out again and vibrantly wings her way
Off along with bag and Chief
Blueshoe on the shopping-mall

Warpath. Don't overdo
It, old geezer with your tremulous tuft
Of chamois hair! *If it weren't so ot,*

Un if I weren't so aold, Oi'd
Be busying moyself wiv evwery secund
Wan ov dem alf-naykid wimmen.

Kiosk, headline: Car stolen
From *right under the bum* of Home
Secretary – sur-

Faced again in Poland. That minister looks
As though you could pull
His chair from under him without him

Noticing, but luckily he's glued
To it as firmly as the gents from the
National team to the pitch

After crashing to defeat against 11
Soccer bananas. Holy
Round-Leather-God, help the sports

Boarding-school and engender handy
Up-and-coming talents not only on the radio
But also in our stadium the

Blind Ballack lookalike with armband
Is advertising some deodorant on the billboard.
                                Too bad they're
Not even fielding him, he's now

Vying in vain for the favour of the
Super-young blondes in their Porsche
Cayennes, high-school graduation date 'zeronine.
                  That Porsche has 380 horse

Power but those Baywatch minxes
Are acting as though they'd enough
Hot stuff themselves, are wearing pink bikinis

Instead of outer garments, and high suede
Boots with wedge heels, well impregnated
At home. They're already looking a little bored

In their scandalous
Lingerie. Meanwhile, a high-school girl,
On a compact course, special subject

History, seems deeply moved on the radio:
When the train with the concentration-camp inmates halts
In the sticks due to engine trouble,

The rumour spreads like wildfire that
The war is over! The young prisoners
Flee, are brutally

Mown down by the SS,
Fifty die. The guy with the inverted
DJ skullcap has tattooed

The arse antlers of his sun-crispy
Girlfriend onto the rear window of his
Japanese limousine and is hightailing out of a

Fitness studio with tyres
Screeching. We too ought to drive back
Now to the country and take a

Cold shower. In the lake there's no
Space left for us, half of Munich
Is swimming around there in its own juice. In the evening,

We'll drive back in to let it all
Hang out. But watch out, people,
Speed-traps are glinting everywhere.

This Cigar

A real hottie
Scrumptious
Mutters the little

Tobacco shop
Girl in her black and white
Mini

Pleated
Skirt and
Promptly

A rocket in your
Trouser pocket
Bukowski

If I had
Polished
Rhymes now

On hand, like
I know something
Else

That'll tickle
Your palate
And the likes of me

Do indeed always
Think of Heinrich
Karl Bukowski

Born 1920
In Andernach
And whatever else

He sputtered about
Went to hell
In L.A.

Scholarly
Alibi
Literary digression

Sinful
Ass-thetics 69
Cents per

Sumatra
Giant Cigarillo
De Olifant

Tinplate
Smoking during
Pregnancy

Harms
Your child
Nine minutes

Nine Months
Life sentence
Schnapps

The idea
To light
One

Was paid for
In a rush
In a puff

Thin
Silk
Stockings, so

Smooth
Shaven
Slippery.

Every Time He Watches Soccer

There's no need for him to sweat;
His better half(pint), a translucent

Blonde, will still appear
In front of him. Once in a while

He yells "Gooal!" or "Damn ya,
You old fat loafer!"

Meantime the missus is fidgeting
In her lonely bed, already dreaming

Of another fella who won't carouse
Every time there's a kick-off.

Death Camp Rosie

This is what the whole village called her, and in my
boyhood days I was wondering why her voice was so deep
and her cheeks sported stubble, old witch style.
Her name, Rosie, or Rosl, had always reminded me

of the *Bräurosl* tent at *Oktoberfest*
until I, still a schoolboy, read about those
white-coat-wearing SS criminals,
portly and prosperous,

 the ones who later got the German Cross of Merit
—or even a papal medal—
pinned on them,
and, of course, some Bavarian awards

on top of that. We even had streets
named after those gangsters! As for Rosie,
she lived her whole life hand to mouth
having got nothing but her small pension,

and she was very unwell, too, trust me;
she no longer could find herself a man,
and for us boys she was nothing else but
an ugly duckling.

Back then, little did we know
about such crazy things as hormone injections,
or whatever they stuffed into her body
as a child. God only knows what she would look like

had she grown up in different circumstances.
These days I am ashamed of that association
with the *Bräurosl* tent, and I can't stop thinking
that we misjudged her character. I also think

of our community's Nazi brass and their offspring:
sons, daughters and grandkids, for whom things are going
swimmingly well; they have little to worry about,
and they hope that God sees them as good people.

Of course, granddad's Nazi medals have long been sold,
and so was his German Cross of Merit;
they visit him once in a while and have a few tulips sent
to lay on his grave, while Rosie's grave has subsided

after only ten years and now has no other adornment
but dandelions, while all the umbrellas flock
around the old Nazi's Carrara marble tombstone.
Ah, Rosie would be amused by that, and I'm amused, too,

as I'm telling you all this.

Mine, Workers

Scraping
Free
Veins

Of words
Syllabic sliver by
Silver.

Anton G. Leitner. Writing in a Brave New World

These *Selected Poems* include works from the early 1980s to the present by the Bavarian poet Anton G. Leitner (more about him here: www.antonleitner.de). This book offers a remarkable occasion to critically review the changing tides in German versification over the last three decades. As the founder and editor of *DAS GEDICHT*, the largest magazine for poetry in the language (also available online at www.dasgedicht.de), as well as a poet in his own right, Anton G. Leitner has been firmly rooted in contemporary German poetry without just simply being its symptom or creature. His writing and his career reveal the struggle of poets for unique rhythm, deportment, and melody in a media environment shifting in its foundations.

"The clock / was drunk / and swung her / pendulum"

At the dawn of the 1980s, the literary field was dominated by a relatively small circle of individuals, a forgone generation, comprised of e.g. Hans Magnus Enzensberger, Friederike Mayröcker, Ernst Jandl, Peter Handke, and Günter Grass. These postwar veterans found their fame in a world that was content with three television channels, all of which were more or less operated by the government. In a world in which the printed book, the textual currency of literature, did not compete with a plethora of YouTube videos and Spotify playlists, they had become household names, as writers, by virtue of an independent press mainly focused on publications released by a dozen or so corporate publishers. In fact, German literary types often referred (and refer) to their scene as the *Literaturbetrieb*, thereby revealing a mindset that envisions all writing, all printing and critical appraising, as part of one large corporate operation: an exclusive tightknit singular business, a cloistered kolkhoz.

This relatively monolithic and ultimately authoritarian organization of the *Literaturbetrieb* started to crumble and fall unto itself as early as the 1980s as new types of poets and literary scene-builders emerged. The history of the past three decades is therefore not the history of the ascending Internet and Social Media surreptitiously undermining the pecuniary basis of publishing, but is the history of individual voices. It is what writing looks like when everyone has a voice.

Enter Anton G. Leitner, born in Munich in 1961. Having published his first poems in an anthology entitled *Füllhorn* (or *Cornucopia*) while still in secondary school at Munich's Wittelsbacher-Gymnasium in 1979/80, he then enrolled as a law student at the Ludwig Maximilian University in his hometown. In the mid-1980s, young Leitner was surrounded by a band of likeminded rivals: the subsequently successful crime novelist Friedrich Ani, the prose provocateur Helmut Krausser, the experimental sound poet Michael Lentz as well as the poet Ulrich Beck. In collaborating and coming together, these young writers founded a society, *die Initative Junger Autoren* (IJA). This organization became a launchpad for literary festivals that they themselves organized as a means of engaging with other literary institutions and as a representative body for their generation of writers. They organized some of the largest readings known in the Bavarian capital at the time, as well as on chartered trains or boats. They also coordinated literary exchange among young writers in East and West Germany on the eve of the German Reunification. In short, they did not ask what the *Literaturbetrieb* could do for them, but put up shop within the *Literaturbetrieb* and made it work for what they had to say. One critic in 1988 noted: "This young movement does not

exhaust its effort in intimate orange tea readings"
(*Tagesspiegel*).

Birth of the Poet Activist

In considering those formative years and events that shaped
the literary biography of Anton G. Leitner, one may easily
perceive the shift that had taken place in the structure of the
Literaturbetrieb. The number of available voices multiplied
significantly. They organized autonomously on local, regional,
and (inter-)national levels, and discovered an arguably more
democratic way to their readership. The entire system of
literary life as we know it today in Europe was born by forces
that first played out among Leitner's generation in Munich
and elsewhere. The advent of Social Media only hastened and
perfected what began with these people in various cities
across the continent. The once jealously and conceitedly
guarded gilded gateway leading to a singular path of letters
was replaced by numerous open avenues, rabbit holes,
wickets, chutes, and catapults that gave access to the realm of
poetry.

Anton G. Leitner's writing should therefore be viewed in the
context of an intensely heightened lust for diversity, variety,
and real interpersonal engagement with writers: the
discovery of themes, images, and experiences as they really
existed in peoples' lives. The literary scene was no longer just
a club of the admirable few, but a labyrinthine network of
scenes, festivals, circles, and sparring magazines – each often
very intimately connected and in touch with their reading
communities. The organization of the literary world as we
know it today was born in that period and Anton G. Leitner
was at the center of its inception. His budding generation
took literature to the grass roots, spelling it out for everyone

to enjoy, poetizing society with a fierce brand of liberal individualism.

Between Editing and Writing

Together with his friend Ludwig Steinherr, the activist poet Anton G. Leitner founded one of the most influential literary magazines in the past quarter century, *DAS GEDICHT*. This magazine, now in its 26th year, is marked by an open mind. Pure and simple. Its editors have the rare ability to see poetry that works well with a general audience, poetry that makes a difference, poetry that matters. The annual print edition has an English-language supplement and a blog featuring a large variety of articles, videos and photographs. Proud of its independence, *DAS GEDICHT* has produced a great number of thematic anthologies. Publishing on topics such as religion, travel, various aspects of sex, political verse, animals, pop culture, or health, Anton G. Leitner has been invited to edit expanded versions of the magazine for major publishers such as Reclam, Goldmann or dtv/Hanser. The literary scholar and critic Hanns-Josef Ortheil once wrote about anthologies edited by Leitner: "Looking at this anthology, I can envision a new beginning for poetry."

The unorthodox combination of well-known established writers and complete newcomers without any credentials whatsoever has brought about a magazine that has been able to find a large audience. Scandals, such as an erotic edition that was refused by some booksellers on grounds of obscenity, naturally, helped to garner public attention. As a result, the list of authors published for the first time or on a regular basis in *DAS GEDICHT* is tantamount to a list of the *Who's Who* in the world of German letters – ranging from Michael Krüger, Reiner Kunze, Ulrike Draesner, Friederike

Mayröcker, Gerhard Rühm to younger poets such as Jan Wagner or Nora Gomringer.

Anton G. Leitner's public interventions, such as having poetry printed on shopping bags or on pouches of sugar, show how much his mind was in line with that of a common man or woman. His poetry takes inspiration from ruckus *Oktoberfest* brawls as much as it sees the comedic tragedy of married life or the twists and contradictions in the patch of German history. He possesses a keen eye for the endearing weirdness of human beings, including his own familial relations, as shown in the poem *Step Forward, Step* about his great-grandfather Josef.

His mode of observation is never cynical but often ironic when casting poetic arrangements. In doing so, Leitner is inherently and strikingly Bavarian: a self-deprecating poet, a gleeful master of the apercu or the surprising right hook, always somewhat at odds with propriety and decorum. Interestingly, Anton G. Leitner has in his more recent work turned to dialectal poetry, verse in his native Bavarian tongue with his widely read book *Schnablgwax* (2016). And while poetry in the Bavarian vernacular often is crude, uncouth, and unsophisticated, Leitner succeeded in combining the technique, reflection, and freshness of 21st century poetics with the tonal pitch of the Southern German local dialect.

This collection affords the reader a broad view of his work in presenting the many masks of this single poet. It offers poetry gleaned from a languorous awareness of tradition alongside works that reflect major political events, such as the fall of the Berlin Wall or the atrocity of the Holocaust.

Paul-Henri Campbell, September 2018

More poetry published by SurVision Books

Noelle Kocot. Humanity
(New Poetics: USA)
ISBN 978-1-9995903-0-7

Ciaran O'Driscoll. The Speaking Trees
(New Poetics: Ireland)
ISBN 978-1-9995903-1-4

Elin O'Hara Slavick. Cameramouth
(New Poetics: USA)
ISBN 978-1-9995903-4-5

Anatoly Kudryavitsky. Stowaway
(New Poetics: Ireland)
ISBN 978-1-9995903-2-1

Christopher Prewitt. Paradise Hammer
(Winner of James Tate Poetry Prize 2018)
ISBN 978-1-9995903-9-0

Bob Lucky. Conversation Starters in the Language No One Speaks
(Winner of James Tate Poetry Prize 2018)
ISBN 978-1-912963-00-3

Sergey Biryukov. Transformations
Translated from Russian
(New Poetics: Russia)
ISBN 978-1-9995903-5-2

Maria Grazia Calandrone. Fossils
Translated from Italian
(New Poetics: Italy)
ISBN 978-1-9995903-6-9

George Kalamaras. That Moment of Wept
ISBN 978-1-9995903-7-6

Our books are available to order via
http://survisionmagazine.com/books.htm

www.ingramcontent.com/pod-product-compliance
Lightning Source LLC
La Vergne TN
LVHW021615080426
835510LV00019B/2590